know
the
game

Basketball

(REVISED EDITION)

Produced for the

AMATEUR BASKET BALL ASSOCIATION

CONTENTS

Foreword

BASKETBALL originated in America, and, like other games that are now styled "national", it started in a humble way. In 1891, Dr. James Naismith conceived the idea of this game when he was a student at the Y.M.C.A. Training College at Springfield, Mass., U.S.A. A peach-basket was erected at each end of the gymnasium and two teams were selected. The object was to get the football that was used into the opponents' basket, using only the hands.

The possibilities of the game soon became apparent and experience led to certain rules being drawn up for the good conduct of the game. As it was not intended to be a kind of indoor rugby, contact with opponents, or tackling in any form, was forbidden. Moreover, the players were not allowed to take more than two steps while in possession of the ball. Thus, skilful passing became—and remains to this day—the chief feature of the play.

At first, this may sound a little tame; but it is no exaggeration to say that Basketball is now one of the most exhilarating and popular indoor games known. It requires absolute fitness, skill, dexterity, co-ordination, agility, alertness and the ability to co-operate with the other members of the team.

So extensive has been the advance of Basketball that it was included in the 1936 Olympiad and has maintained its place ever since. It is now played in over 100 countries, in many of which it has surpassed the popularity of soccer, baseball and other "national" games. Though not so well known in this country at present, it is fast approaching that end.

The governing association in this country was founded in 1935, and has organised and entered teams in many international events including the Olympic Games.

For clubs wishing to take part in local and national leagues and tournaments it is essential to be affiliated to the national governing body.

Herbert Naylor

Founder and (late) Chairman,
Amateur Basket Ball Association.

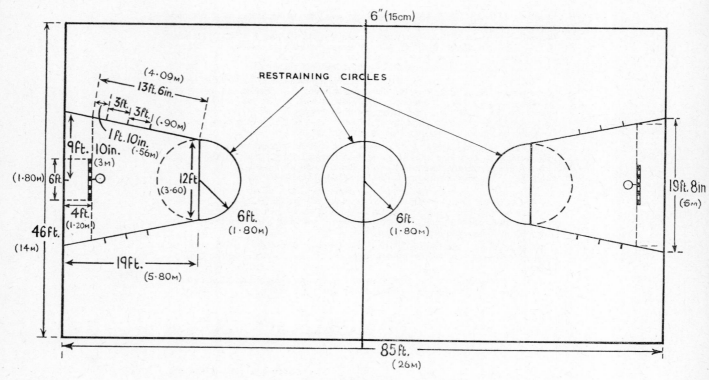

6" (15cm)

RESTRAINING CIRCLES

(4·09m)
13ft. 6in.

3ft. 3ft. (·90m)

1 ft. 10 in.
(·56m)

9ft. 10in.
(3m)

(1·80m) 6ft.

12ft
(3·60)

6ft.
(1·80m)

6ft.
(1·80m)

4ft.
(1·20m)

19ft. 8in
(6m)

46ft.
(14m)

19ft.
(5·80m)

85ft.
(26m)

The Basketball Court

The Game

The aim of each team is to throw the ball into its opponents' basket (i.e., the one they are attacking), and to prevent the other team from securing the ball or scoring. The visiting team has the choice of ends.

The game is started by a "Jump ball" at the centre when the referee throws the ball up.

When the ball is in play it may be passed, thrown, rolled, batted or dribbled in any direction. Quick passing is the best way to get the ball into a scoring position.

A player must not carry the ball for more than one pace.

The game is stopped when certain rules are infringed.

The most important rule is that concerning personal contact — a player must avoid contact with other players. If contact (which could have been avoided) occurs a "personal foul" is recorded against the fouler. His opponents restart the game by a throw-in from the side-line unless the foul was intentional or was inflicted on a player in the act of shooting.

In these instances free throws will be given, or a choice of free throws or a throw-in from midway 'on the side line.

Time lost during all stoppages is allowed for.

The game is divided into two periods of twenty minutes each, with a half-time interval of ten minutes.

A game cannot end in a draw. An extra period of five minutes is played plus as many more periods necessary to break the tie. Teams toss for first choice of ends and change ends after each extra period.

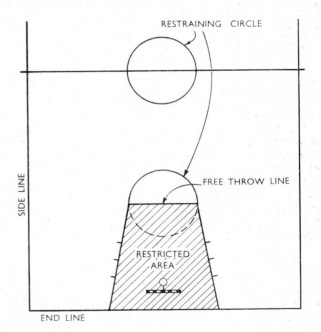

The Playing Court

Basketball is played on a court marked out on a flat surface; grass courts are not allowed.

The usual measurements are 85 feet (26 m) long and 46 feet (14 m) wide, but a variation is allowed of 6 ft. 6 in. (2 m) on the length and 3 ft. 3 in. (1 m) on the width, although the court must be in the correct proportion length to width.

All lines should be painted 2 inches (5 cm) wide.

Equipment

THE BASKETS

The baskets are best made of white-cord net, which should be so constructed as to check the fall of the ball. They hang from iron rings which are fixed 10 feet (3·05 m) above the floor. The rings are painted orange.

Each basket is 18 inches (45·0 cm) across at the top and 16 inches (40 cm) deep, tapering slightly towards the bottom, which is open. A goal is scored when the ball enters the basket from above and remains in or passes through it.

THE BACKBOARDS

The backboard prevents the ball from going out of play during shots at the basket. Its measurements are 6 feet (1·8 m) by 4 feet (1·20 m), usually made of smooth hard wood $1\frac{3}{16}$ inches thick but can be trans-

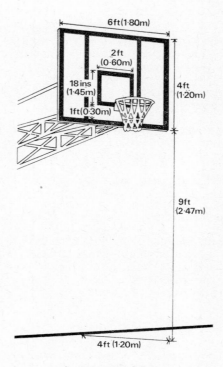

Basket and Backboard

parent. Its face should be white with a black border and the smaller rectangle marked on it should be black. Where transparent boards are used, the markings are in white.

The lower edge of the backboard is 1 foot below the edge of the basket ring and the board itself must be 4 feet (1·20 m) inside the court. This overhang may be reduced in certain instances, but in all cases the free-throw line must be 15 feet (4·57 m) from the plane of the backboard.

THE BALL

The ball must be between 29½ inches (75 cm) and 31½ inches (78 cm) in circumference. Its weight should be at least 21.6 ozs. (600 g) but not more than 22.92 ozs. (650 g).

It should be so inflated that if it is dropped on a wooden floor from a height of 6 feet (1.80 m), it will bounce to a height of 4 feet (1·20 m) to 4 feet 8 inches (1·40 m) measured to the top of the ball.

THE DRESS

Players are recommended to wear shorts and vests.

Singlets are the recognised form of dress. Jerseys are not acceptable. The answer to body cooling control is a track suit. The boots are very important and special basketball boots should be worn if possible, although soft gym shoes are quite suitable. They

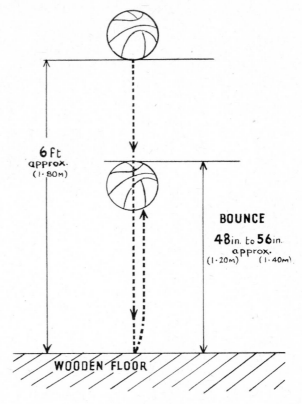

6 ft approx. (1·80M)

BOUNCE
48 in. to 56 in. approx.
(1·20m) (1·40m)

WOODEN FLOOR

The Ball Test

should fit well and, for comfort, two pairs of socks are advised.

Each player must be numbered on the front (4 inches (10 cm) high) and back (8 inches (20 cm)) of his vest. Numbers range from 4 to 15 inclusive.

The Teams

The game is played by two teams. Each team has five players and is allowed five substitutes. The coach of each team must see that the scorer knows the players' names and numbers.

SUBSTITUTIONS

Any or all of the five players in action may be replaced by substitutes during the game. This is done on instructions by the team's coach, assistant coach, or by its captain if the coaches are not present, but the selected substitute must remain outside the court until one of the officials beckons him. He gives the scorer his name and number before going on the court. Substitutions can only be made when the ball is 'dead' and the game clock stopped.

Following a violation, only the team who has possession of the ball for the Throw-in from out of bounds may effect a substitution. If this occurs the opponents also may effect a substitution.

The only members of a team allowed to speak to an official during the game are the captain and a substitute when reporting the number of the player he is replacing.

The basic positions are comparatively unimportant in basketball owing to the fluid nature of the game and the many stratagems employed. The basic principle is that every player should be able to fulfil all functions. There is no off-side rule.

Starting Play

Play is started by a jump ball in the centre.

JUMP BALL

One member of each team stands at the centre on either side of the line marked across the circle.

All other players must remain outside the restraining circle until the jump ball has been completed; and two team-mates must not stand next to each other if an opponent claims one of their positions.

The referee tosses the ball up in such a way that it would drop on the centre line between the two participating players if they were to let it. As the ball reaches its highest point, which must be higher than the players can reach by jumping; they may jump for it and tap it by hand, in any direction, while it is dropping.

They must not leave their positions until one of them has touched the ball. Neither of them may tap it more than twice; and the player who has touched it twice may not do so again until the ball has touched one of the players who was outside the circle, the basket or the backboard, or the floor.

Jump Ball

Catching the Ball

Pivoting sharply to pass the ball in a direction not anticipated by his opponents

Dribbling

In Play

A PLAYER

(a) May *catch, control, pass* or *shoot* the ball with either or both of his hands.

(b) May *dribble* the ball by throwing, batting, bouncing or rolling it. He may begin a dribble by tossing the ball into the air and touching it again before it hits the floor, thereafter it must always touch the floor before he handles it again. The dribble ends when he touches the ball with both hands at once or allows it to rest in either or both hands.

(c) May *carry* the ball for one complete pace, but not for two or more paces.

(d) May *shoot* and *score* from any point in the court.

(e) May *pivot* with the ball in his hands. That is, he can *step once or more* in any direction with one foot while turning on the other, which must stay on the floor at its point of contact.

(i) If he receives the ball when standing still he can pivot with either foot.

One count occurs (a) when he receives the ball if one foot is on the floor or (b) when one, or both feet simultaneously, touch the floor if he was in the air when he caught the ball.

"One-count"   "Two-count"

(ii) If he receives the ball whilst moving, he may use a two-count rhythm in coming to a stop or in passing the ball; but after "two-count", only the rear foot may be used as the pivot unless the feet are level, in which case either foot may be used as the pivot foot.

Two-count occurs when, after count "one", either foot touches the floor again or both feet touch the floor simultaneously.

(iii) The pivot foot may be lifted to pass or shoot provided the ball is released before the foot touches the floor again. The pivot foot may not be lifted when starting a dribble until the ball has left the player's hand.

Not Allowed

A PLAYER

(a) Must not *hit* the ball with clenched fist.

(b) Must not *kick* the ball, i.e. *deliberately* play it with his foot.

(c) Must not *carry* the ball for more than one pace.

(d) Must not "*double dribble*". This means that when he has ended a dribble he must not begin another until he has made a shot or has lost possession of the ball.

(e) Must not remain in the restricted area for more than 3 seconds when he or his team has control of the ball, unless he himself begins to dribble for a shot at goal.

(f) Must not take more than 5 seconds to put the ball into play when an official assigns this duty to him.

(g) Must not be guilty of "Personal Contact". See "Fouls".

(h) Must not be guilty of "Technical Fouls". See "Fouls".

(i) A team in possession of the ball must make an attempt at the basket within 30 seconds of having gained control.

(j) The attacking team must get the ball into its front court within 10 seconds and then not pass it back again. This includes from a throw-in awarded in the front court.

Penalty

For any of the infringements **(a)** to **(f)** and including **(i)** the offender's opponents are awarded a throw-in which takes place at the side-line at that point out of bounds which is nearest the spot where the offence occurred.

Fouls

PERSONAL CONTACT

Every player *must* by all reasonable means avoid contact with an opponent, but if this occurs, a personal foul is awarded against the player whom the official considers to be primarily responsible.

BLOCKING

Blocking is personal contact hindering the progress of an opponent who has *not* got the ball. A player can take up any position on the court not occupied by another player, but he must not be so close as to interfere with the opponent's normal movements (approx. 3 feet (90 cm) away).

The player who does this is guilty of a personal foul, unless his opponent resorts to deliberate pushing, charging, or holding.

One or more players are allowed to run down the court close to a team-mate who has the ball, to prevent opponents from approaching him. But if they run into an

Accidental Contact

Blocking

opponent who has taken up a position in their path, *they are guilty of charging or "blocking"*.

A player who tries to dribble between two opponents, or between an opponent and a boundary line, when he has no reasonable chance of getting through without personal contact, is guilty of a personal foul if contact occurs.

Penalty for personal foul

A player who fouls an opponent has the foul charged against him. The offender *must raise his arm and turn to face the table*, so that the scorer may record the foul correctly. For failing to do this, the offending player, after being warned once by an official, may have a technical foul charged against him.

A player who has committed *five* fouls, personal *or* technical, must leave the court.

The non-offending team is given the ball for a throw-in from out of bounds at the side-line nearest the place of the foul (see Technical Foul), unless the foul was committed on a player in the act of shooting, or was an intentional foul.

FOUL ON PLAYER SHOOTING FOR GOAL

If the shot is successful no free throws are awarded. If unsuccessful, two free throws are awarded, or the option of a throw-in from the mid-point side line.

INTENTIONAL FOUL

If the foul is intentional two free throws are awarded or the option of a throw-in from the mid-point side-line except when a goal is scored by the offended player.

A multiple foul is when a player is fouled by two or more opponents at the same moment. A personal foul is charged against each offender and the offended player shall be awarded two free throws or the option of a throw-in from the mid-point side line. If he is in the act of shooting, the goal, if made, shall count and no free throws will be awarded, but the fouls shall be charged against the foulers. The ball is brought into play from behind the end line.

A **double** foul is a situation where two opponents commit personal fouls against each other at the same moment. No free throws are awarded but a foul is charged against each offending player. The ball is brought into play at the nearest circle by a jump ball between the two players involved.

TECHNICAL FOULS

Technical fouls may be offences against the spirit of the game but some, which are obviously unintentional and have no effect on the play, or are of an administrative nature, are not considered technical fouls unless there is repetition *after* a warning by an official.

Technical infractions which are deliberate, or unsportsmanlike, or which give the offender an unfair advantage are penalised immediately with a technical foul.

A player shall not disregard warnings by an official or use unsportsmanlike actions such as:

(a) Delaying the game by preventing the ball from being put promptly into play.
(b) Baiting an opponent or handicapping him by waving hands close to his eyes.
(c) Using profanity or disrespectfully addressing an official.
(d) Not raising his arm properly when charged with a foul.
(e) Changing his number without telling the scorer and the referee. Neither shall he enter the court as a substitute without reporting first to the scorer and then to an official.

Penalty for a player technical foul

Each offence will be charged against the offender and two free throws awarded to the opponents or the option of a throw-in from the mid-point side line. The captain shall designate the thrower. For infractions which are persistent or flagrant a player shall be disqualified.

Technical foul
by coach or substitute

Neither coach, assistant coach nor substitute player may enter the court without permission. None may leave their places to follow, or disrespectfully address officials (including Table officials) or opponents.

During a charged time-out a coach may address his players, including substitutes, providing each keeps to his legitimate side of the boundary line.

Here again a distinction is made between *unintentional* and *deliberate* infractions by coaches or substitute.

Penalty

Each offence by the coach shall be recorded and *one* free throw awarded to the opponents. After the free throw, whether successful or not, the ball is put into play, at mid-court side-line, by a member of the free thrower's team. Persistent or flagrant infraction may cause him to be banished from the vicinity of the court. The assistant coach, or if none, the captain, would then replace him as coach.

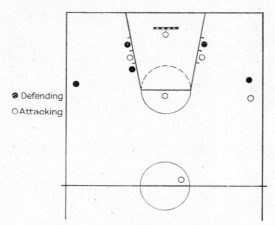

● Defending
○ Attacking

During a free throw, each player positions himself according to the tactics adopted by his team

Free Throws and their Sequels

A free throw for a *personal* foul goes to the player who was fouled unless he is disqualified for any reason, or injured. For a *technical* foul, the throw may be made by any member of the team to which it has been granted. Free throws are made from inside the semi-circle. The thrower stands immediately behind (not on) the free throw line.

Nobody — not even an official — may stand inside the free throw lane when a player is making a free throw:

Taking the Free Throw

and there must be no lining up along the sides of the lane when this follows a coach technical foul. In other cases, the players may stand just outside the lane in the spaces marked. The spaces nearer the basket are for two players of the defending team. The other players take alternate positions.

The free thrower is allowed a maximum of 5 seconds for his shot. He must not touch the line or the court beyond the free throw line until the ball touches the ring or the basket or the backboard, or until it is apparent it will not touch either.

FREE THROW RESULT	SEQUEL AFTER A SECOND THROW FOR PERSONAL FOUL OR PLAYER TECHNICAL FOUL	SEQUEL AFTER A COACH TECHNICAL FOUL
Free throw is successful	Throw-in from behind end line by any member of the free thrower's opponents	Throw-in from side-line at mid-court by any member of the free thrower's team
Free throw fails—ball hits the ring and drops into the court	Ball remains in play	
Free throw fails—ball does not hit basket-ring or backboard, but goes out of bounds	Throw in from side-line nearest that point by any member of the free thrower's opponents	
Free throw fails—ball does not hit basket-ring or backboard but drops inside the court		
If a member of the free thrower's team violates the line and (i) Free thrower scores (ii) Free thrower fails to score	(i) Basket will count. Throw-in from end line by opponents. (ii) Opponents throw-in from side line opposite free throw line	
Free thrower's opponents break any of the free throw rules (i) Free thrower scores (ii) Free thrower fails to score	(i) Offence by opponents ignored. Basket will count (ii) Free thrower granted another free throw under similar conditions	
If members of both teams violate the line	Basket counts if scored. Violation is disregarded. If free throw is missed play is resumed by a jump ball at the nearest restraining circle	
Free thrower has broken any of the free throw rules. Thus he cannot score and the ball is "dead"	Throw-in from side line by any member of free thrower's opponents	Throw-in from side-line at centre by any member of free thrower's team

Out of Bounds

The ball is out of bounds:

(a) when it touches a player who is out of bounds—i.e. a player touching the floor on or outside the boundary line and that player is held responsible.

(b) when it touches any other person, the floor or any object on or outside the boundary, or the supports or back of the backboard. It is considered to have been put out of bounds by the player who last touched it.

An official then indicates the team who are to put the ball into play, a player of which stands out of bounds near the point where the ball left the court, and within five seconds from the time the ball is at his disposal, he must throw, bounce, or roll it to another player within the court. The ball must be handed by the official to the player who is to put it into play if the out of bounds is in that half of the court containing his opponent's basket. While the ball is being passed into the court, every other player must be completely inside the court.

On courts where the margin of "out of bounds" is less than three feet, no player from either team is allowed to be within three feet of the man putting the ball into play.

Note.—If the ball goes out of bounds:—

(a) after being touched simultaneously by two opponents.

(b) when the official is doubtful who last touched the ball.

(c) when the officials disagree.

play is restarted by a jump ball between the two players concerned at the nearest restraining circle.

Restarting Play

We have already described how play is restarted after most interruptions. The commonest method is the throw-in from out of bounds, e.g., see page 18.

After a field goal play is restarted by an opponent of the scoring team by throwing the ball into court from behind the end line where the goal was scored. The ball must be returned into play within five seconds after it is first handed to or taken up by a player behind the line.

S I D E   L I N E

Touching the ball simultaneously

Dead Ball

The ball is "dead", meaning that it is out of play, during any official interruption of the game. It becomes "Alive" again:

(a) when tapped at a jump ball;

(b) when placed at the disposal of a free thrower;

(c) when touched by a player on the court after a throw-in.

Held Ball

This may be declared:—

(a) when two or more rival players have the ball locked between their hands or bodies so that neither of them, nor any other player, can get it away without using "undue roughness".

(b) when any single player closely guarded is holding the ball and does not put the ball in play within 5 seconds.

(c) when the ball lodges in the basket supports.

After calling a "held ball", the referee orders a "jump ball" between the two rival players concerned. This jump ball takes place at the centre of the nearest restraining circle.

"Held-Ball"

Time-out

The game clock is stopped for time out when an official signals:

(a) a violation;

(b) a foul;

(c) a jump ball;

(d) unusual delay in getting a dead ball into play;

(e) suspension of play for injury or for removal of a player, or for any reason ordered by the officials;

(f) when the 30-second signal is sounded.

In addition teams are allowed two "time-out" periods, each of one minute duration, in each half, for consultation on tactics, etc. These can be requested when the ball is dead and the game clock stopped (as listed above).

When the introduction of a substitute takes more than 20 seconds the delay is counted as a time-out and charged to the offending team.

TEN SECOND RULE

The attacking team must bring the ball to its front court within 10 seconds from the moment it has got possession of the ball in court. The same team cannot pass the ball to its back court. This restriction applies to all situations including throw-in from out of bounds, rebounds and interceptions. It does not apply, however, to jump ball at the centre circle, or the situation when the captain uses his option of taking the throw-in from the mid-point on the side line instead of taking the free throws.

Scoring

Scoring is by a system of points.

Two points are awarded for a "goal from the field", i.e., when the ball drops into the basket as a result of ordinary play.

One point is awarded for a goal scored by a free throw.

If a team refuses to continue to play after being so ordered by the referee it forfeits the game. The opponents are credited with a 2-0 win unless they were leading by a different score in which case the greater score stands.

If there is any interference with the basket, during an attempt at goal, points may be awarded, thus:—

Suppose the ball is resting on the ring during an attempt at a goal, and at that moment, a defender touches the *net* or *backboard*. The ball immediately becomes "dead" and the thrower is awarded two points if the throw was from the field or one point if it was a free throw.

A defender may not touch the ball, after it has started on its downward flight, whilst the ball is completely above the level of the basket ring. This restriction applies only to a throw (not a "batted" ball), and only until the thrown ball touches the ring or it is apparent it will not touch it.

An *attacker* who touches the *basket* when attempting to play a ball resting on the ring, after a shot from the field, commits a violation.

The ball is declared "dead", no points can be scored, and the defenders put the ball in from out of bounds at the side line opposite the spot.

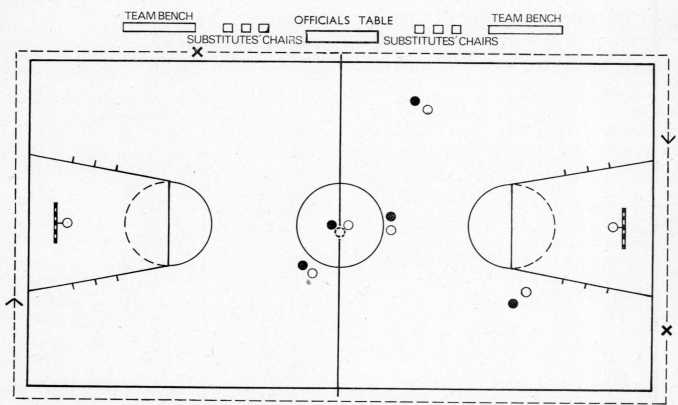

TEAM BENCH   OFFICIALS TABLE   TEAM BENCH

SUBSTITUTES' CHAIRS   SUBSTITUTES' CHAIRS

After "jump ball", the referee and the umpire, "X", remain behind the sidelines,
both moving with the game as indicated in the diagram by the broken lines

Page Twenty-two

Control of the Game

OFFICIALS

A game is supervised by a referee and an umpire who are known as the officials, assisted by a timekeeper and a scorer. They are required to wear white basketball shoes, light grey trousers and grey shirt.

The referee is responsible for:—

(a) inspection and approval of all equipment.

(b) tossing the ball at the centre to start play.

(c) deciding whether a goal shall count.

(d) a team's forfeiture of a game when conditions warrant it.

(e) deciding questions on which timekeeper and scorer disagree.

(f) examining the score book and approving the score at the end of each half.

(g) making decisions on any points not covered by the rules.

The referee and the umpire jointly conduct the game according to the rules.

Their duties include:—

(a) putting the ball into play.

(b) deciding when the ball becomes dead.

(c) stopping play when the ball is dead.

(d) ordering or allowing time-out.

(e) beckoning substitutes on to the court.

(f) passing the ball to a player for a specified throw from a prescribed position.

(g) counting seconds when a player must play the ball or shoot within a time-limit.

The officials are also responsible for imposing penalties for breaches of the rules and for unsportsmanlike conduct.

Play is stopped by one of the officials blowing a whistle when a decision has to be made known. Time-out may be ordered if a player is injured.

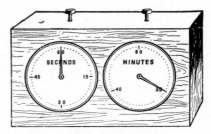

Game Clock

THE TIMEKEEPER

The timekeeper, who sits off the court, must have at least one stop-watch (called the game clock). The clock records both the playing time and the time of stoppages as provided for in the rules.

He must give the referee more than three minutes notice before each half so that the referee can give the teams a clear three minutes warning before the start of play. The timekeeper must also signal to the scorer two minutes before starting time, and indicate the end of playing time in each half or extra period "with gong, pistol or bell".

THE SCORER

The scorer is required to:—

(a) record the names and numbers of all players taking part in a game, and inform the nearer official if there is any breach of the rules about the numbers and substitution of players.

(b) keep a tally of the points scored by each player and team (see "Scoring", page 21).

(c) note all fouls, personal and technical, and tell an official immediately when a player has committed a total of five fouls.

(d) record the time-outs debited to each team, and warn a team through an official when it has had four of these (two in either half). A team may have one further time-out in each extra period.

The Score Sheet

SIGNALS

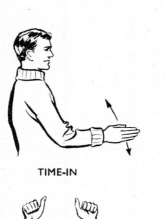

TIME-IN

OFFICIALS TIME-OUT

CHARGED TIME-OUT

SUBSTITUTION

JUMP BALL

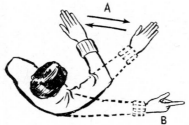

**VIOLATION,
OUT OF BOUNDS
A: violations signal
B: direction of play**

TRAVELLING

ILLEGAL DRIBBLE

3 SECONDS RULE INFRACTION

CANCEL SCORE

PERSONAL FOUL

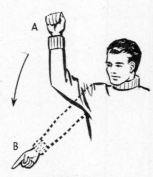

PERSONAL FOUL
No free throws
(Finger pointing to sideline)

FREE THROWS PENALTY

TECHNICAL FOUL

DOUBLE FOUL

INTENTIONAL FOUL

HOLDING

PUSHING

CHARGING

ILLEGAL USE OF HANDS
Strike wrist

TO DESIGNATE OFFENDER
Hold up number of player

SCORE COUNTS
(One finger - one point)

DURING FREE THROWS
Signal two throws

DURING FREE THROWS
Signal one throw

ADVICE ON PLAY

Like other games that have become popular throughout the world basketball in its basic form is a simple game. It is a team passing game in which the object is to score a goal, each team endeavouring to prevent their opponents gaining possession of the ball or scoring. The basic rules are that the ball must be played by hand; a player may not run carrying the ball although he may move from one spot to another using a dribble and finally, and most important of all, there shall be no physical contact between players.

Beginners and experienced players need to remind themselves that basketball has this simple basis; good players and leading teams are those who can perform the simple skills very well. Although the game is simple to play, to master it requires practice on the part of individual players and the team.

The basic fundamental skills of the game are:
(a)   Passing and catching
(b)   Shooting
(c)   Dribbling
(d)   Footwork
(e)   Individual Offence
(f)   Individual Defence

These individual skills have to be worked into a team's method of attack — their team offence — and their team defence.

Passing and Catching

A successful pass is one made between team-mates when the ball is received by the catcher at the point where he requires it. This requires good passing on the part of the passer, recognition of the opening and opportunity to pass by the passer and the execution of the pass quickly and accurately, and of course the receiver must be ready to catch the ball.

CATCHING

1. Make a target with your hands for the passer to aim at.
2. Keep your eyes on the ball.
3. When receiving the ball catch it with the fingers spread and cushion it in by bending the arms.
4. Endeavour to get the ball under control in two hands as quickly as possible so you can shoot, dribble or pass.

PASSING

1. Start with two hands on the ball.
2. Hold the ball firmly but comfortably in the fingers keeping the palms of the hands away from the ball. Obtain full control of the ball before passing.
3. Keep your passing simple, never use fancy passes.
4. Pass under a big person and over a small one.
5. Never pass blind; pass where you are looking and look where you are passing.

6. Use a strong finger and wrist action to pass the ball, follow through.

7. Govern the speed and direction of your pass to movements of your team-mate.

8. Do not force your passes, keep your passes short, snappy and to the target — the chest is the best target. Avoid long cross-court passes.

The main passes used in the game are:

Chest pass This is the most important and the basic pass of the game. From a position with the ball held in two hands at the chest with the fingers alongside the ball and thumbs behind, the ball is passed by fully extending the arms, snapping the wrist and pushing the ball with the fingers. Relax the elbows and extend the arms to follow through fully.

Passing

Bounce pass   This is an effective pass to use when an opponent is between the passer and his team-mate, particularly when the opponent is tall. The passer uses the same action as in the chest pass except the ball is directed towards the ground so that it will skid towards the receiver. The ball should hit the ground about two-thirds of the distance to the receiver and should be kept at knee height. This pass is slow and therefore easy for an opponent to intercept.

Two hand overhead pass   This is an excellent pass for the tall player to use when passing over a smaller player. The ball is taken up in two hands to a position above the head (as in diagram) and from this position is passed using a vigorous snap of the wrist and fingers to pass the ball directly to a team-mate.

One hand javelin pass   This is the pass to use over a long distance. Using the javelin throwing action the ball is passed with one hand quickly to a team-mate. The passer takes the ball back behind the head, turning his body and then throws the ball following through with the throwing hand to ensure maximum accuracy and to prevent the ball from spinning.

Hand-off pass   When a team-mate is cutting close to the ball handler a short hand-off pass is used. In this pass the ball is put into the air so that the cutting player can take the ball as soon as possible after the ball leaves the passer's hand.

Two Hand Overhead Pass

Shooting

To win games a team must be able to score goals; as every player in Basketball is permitted to shoot and score, every player must be a scoring threat. To perfect the skill of shooting, good technique and lots of practice of this good technique are required.

To be a successful shooter a player must:

1. Be on balance when taking the shot. Any movement should be up and down on the spot or towards the basket.
2. Control the ball. The best grip is in two hands with the fingers comfortably spread. Grip the ball with the fingers and the top of the palm, keeping the rest of the palm away from the ball. Grip the ball firmly but not tightly. Keep the ball close to the body.
3. Concentrate on the target — the ring — throughout the shot. Keep the eyes on the target until the ball goes through the ring.
4. Shoot the ball using a wrist and finger action with a strong follow through no matter what type of shot is used. The ball should be shot into the air so that it drops down into the basket.
5. Be relaxed when taking the shot. Good players make their shooting seem easy. To develop this ability, take a shot only when you have a chance to get on balance to control yourself and the ball. Don't rush the shot. When in doubt don't shoot.

One Hand Set Shot

The three basic shots are:

One hand set shot (see page 31). In this shot the Player, with the ball in both hands, takes the ball up in front of his face to above his head turning the ball so that the shooting hand is behind and slightly under the ball. As the ball comes up above head height the support hand is released and the shooting hand releases the ball from the fingertips with a strong wrist action following

through with the arm and straightening the legs so that there is movement towards the basket. Most players maintain a continuous movement from the time they start the shot until the release.

Lay-up shot This is a shot taken at the end of a run in which the player takes a high jump to get close to the basket to give himself the shortest possible distance to shoot the ball. Shooting the ball from the right hand side of the basket, the ball is taken as the right foot comes down to the ground. The player continues his run and takes off from his left foot, jumping as high as possible. The ball is taken up in front of his face and the shot taken from the right hand at the top of the jump and at full stretch. The ball is laid softly against the backboard so that it drops easily into the basket. Young players should also master this shot from the left hand side when the ball should be shot from the left hand taking off for the shot from the right foot. This shot demands a definite "One-two" rhythm for correct execution.

Jump shot (See page 36). This is the most popular shot with top class players. The shot is taken, usually following a dribble, when the player stops with feet close together, gathers himself and then jumps straight up. As he jumps the ball is taken up in front of his face to a position above the head with the shooting hand behind and slightly under the ball. From this position the ball is shot with a vigorous wrist and finger action at the top of the jump.

Lay-up Shot

Dribbling

As in passing and shooting the wrist and fingers are used in dribbling. Keeping the palm off the ball, the fingers push the ball into the ground. Keep the ball low, bend the knees and upper body but keep the head up so that the ball is dribbled away from the feet. Once the player has mastered the touch of the dribble he must dribble using feel only so he can dribble and at the same time see movements by team-mates and opponents. Some inexperienced players get into the habit of bouncing the ball once every time they receive a pass. This prevents another dribble and limits the individual offensive movements of these players. Good dribblers can change direction and speed and through these manoeuvres often beat an opponent.

Footwork

The inexperienced player must master the "One-two" rhythm (see page 12) in coming to a stop with the ball or in passing and shooting. This rhythm together with the pivot is the basis of all basketball footwork. It is essential that the stops and pivot should be used as part of a natural moving action, i.e., as part of a run or walk.

Individual Offence

Although basketball is a team game a team's success will depend a great deal on the ability of each player on court being able to beat his opponent, whether it be in shooting and scoring over the defender; making a successful pass although marked; being able to beat an opponent by deception, both with and without the ball, to receive a pass or to make an easier shot. When being marked closely by an opponent the offensive player with the ball usually uses his dribble or a fake followed by a dribble to beat his man. The offensive player uses a fake to force the defender to make a mistake, e.g., jump to check a faked shot or commit himself to a move in one direction and then the offensive player takes advantage of the opening this has made. The main deceptive moves are foot fakes or a feinted movement with the ball or body. The illustration on page 34 shows a player (No. 8) faking to his right with the defender falling into the trap and moving in that direction and then the offensive player drives to the left through the opening he has made.

Individual Defence

Not only must an individual player be able to beat an opponent on offence but he must be able to defend. A good basketball team has a sound defence. In order to play good individual defence a player should apply certain basic principles, which are:

1   Position — always be between your opponent and the basket he is attacking.

2. Stance — on balance with knees slightly bent, feet spread comfortably with the weight over the balls of the feet, head up and seat down.

3. Footwork — good footwork enables the defender to maintain his position. The basic footwork is a boxer's shuffle, that is, the feet are slid along the ground, if the right foot moves then the left foot follows it but never passes it.

4. Armwork — when your man receives the ball the hands are used as an additional defensive weapon.

With arms slightly bent, one hand is up and forward to discourage the shot and the other hand is out to the side to cover the dribble or bounce pass.

5. Aggression — without hustle and drive on the part of the defender the application of the other principles will be far less effective. The defender must watch his opponent. The best point on which to fix the eyes is the waist; this will help prevent being misled by head or foot fakes. Watch the opponent and consider his play, his weaknesses and strong

Fake and Drive

points and adapt your defensive play to your opponent. The defender must drive himself to work hard when on defence.

Rebounding

Possession is the most important factor in basketball — remember a team can score only when it has the ball. When a shot is missed obtaining the rebound is vital whether your team is on defence or offence. Once the shot is taken obtaining a good position under the backboard must be stressed. This position should not be directly under the backboard but sufficiently in front to allow the ball to bounce from the board. On defence you should endeavour to take up a position between your man and the basket — block him out and then go for the ball. Although defensive players usually start with the best position for the rebound offensive, players must make every effort to beat the defender to the best rebound position. Most important, players must learn to time their jump so that the ball is caught at the top of the jump.

Team Play

Basketball is a team game and it is the 5 players working together as a unit on offence and defence that produces the best results. There are many different systems of play used in basketball, but whatever system your team employs it is most important that all 5 players work together.

Defensive Stance

Jump Shot

TEAM OFFENCE

The object of the team play on offence is to free a player for an easy shot. This may be achieved by:

    (a)   a fast break, i.e., the offence aims to move the ball quickly from defence into a shooting position before the defence gets set.

    (b)   a set offence. In this method of offence the team stations the players in a definite balanced attacking formation. From the formation either individual players will beat an opponent and take the shot or 2 or 3 players will work together to free a team-mate for a shot. The best formation is with players well spaced out to allow room for players to free themselves without one defender being able to mark two attacking players. Basic team offence usually involves the use of:

    (a)   movements that encourage the defenders to make a mistake. These usually involve the offensive players in using individual offensive tactics such as change of direction or fakes, or

    (b)   screens, in which a team-mate attempts to prevent a defender following the offensive man he is marking. In the illustration player No. 12 has set a screen from behind which a team-mate is taking a jump shot.

TEAM DEFENCE

For a sound team defence it is even more important that the 5 players work as a team. Team play on defence enables a team to cover individual weaknesses on defence or strength of the offence. There are two main patterns of team defence — "Man-to-Man" or "Zone". (Both these defences employ good individual defence).

In "Man-to-Man" defence each player is responsible for one particular opponent and endeavours to prevent this player scoring and whenever possible from gaining possession of the ball.

In "Zone" defence the defenders are still concerned with individual players but players move in their zone in relation to the position of the ball. This type of defence requires more team work and excellent individual defence by players and is most effective against a team of poor shooters.

Printed in Great Britain by Terry & Nephew Ltd., Dewsbury